THE SEA

Sea Pink (watercolour)
SARAH FOX-DAVIES

William Green.
Hill Top.

The Sea
A CELEBRATION

Edited by Peter Wood

Masked butterfly fish in the Red Sea, Egypt
LINDA PITKIN

David & Charles

A DAVID & CHARLES BOOK

All contributors retain copyright in their
individual pieces.
This anthology © David & Charles 1993
First published 1993

All rights reserved. No part of this
publication may be reproduced, stored in
a retrieval system, or transmitted, in any
form or by any means, electronic or
mechanical, by photocopying, recording
or otherwise, without prior permission in
writing from the publisher.

A catalogue record for this book is
available from the British Library.

ISBN 0 7153 0036 9

Designed by Jonathan Newdick
Typeset in Spectrum 556 by August
Filmsetting, Haydock, St Helens
and printed in Singapore by
CS Graphics Pte Ltd
for David & Charles
Brunel House Newton Abbot Devon

To Lisa, who attempts to swim against the flow

SANDWELL LIBRARY
& INFORMATION
SERVICE

I 2046127

Gift   9. 6. 11

704.9437

CONTENTS

Grey Reef Shark taken in the Red Sea
JEREMY STAFFORD-DEITSCH

Acknowledgements

Many people have assisted in the completion of this book. I would like to take this opportunity to thank everyone at David & Charles for their foresight in publishing such an exciting project; Charlotte Grimshaw, Laura Mackenzie, Barbara Finnis, Annie Gould and all at Greenpeace for their help and for being there when we ALL need them; Michael Spender (Royal Society of Painters in Watercolours), Arena and The Organisation; the publicity departments at David & Charles, Walker Books, BBC Books and other publishers who have helped to contact the artists.

Finally and most importantly the biggest thank you must go to all the contributors who have given so generously to portray the beauty and wonder of the sea.

Sea stacks, St Kilda (an aquatint)
NORMAN ACKROYD

7

The Work of Greenpeace

Greenpeace has pioneered environmental campaigning on the high seas and their many campaigns have brought the plight of the seas into the homes of millions of people worldwide via television, radio and newspapers.

Greenpeace campaigns against environmental abuse through non-violent direct actions, bearing witness to environmental destruction, identifying those responsible and alerting people everywhere to the problem. Greenpeace's direct actions aim to halt the destruction, if only temporarily, and by showing that the environment can be protected, create sufficient public pressure to ensure permanent change. However, the success of every Greenpeace campaign also depends on careful research and persistent, effective lobbying of governments and international conventions. All Greenpeace campaigns are backed up by extensive scientific research.

First formed when a group of North American activists sailed a small boat into the US atomic test zone off Amchitka, Alaska, back in 1971, Greenpeace still abides by the same principles that triggered the first action. Determined individuals can alter the actions and purposes of even the overwhelmingly powerful by drawing attention to and preventing environmental abuse through their unwavering presence, whatever the risk. As a result, politicians have acted to save whales, ban sea dumping of toxic wastes and, indeed, protect the entire continent of Antarctica.

By 1979, offices had opened in Australia, Canada, France, the Netherlands, New Zealand, the UK and USA.

These Greenpeace entities formed the original Greenpeace International, which is the co-ordinating body between the national offices. Greenpeace now operates in thirty countries; recently offices have been opened in Russia, the Ukraine, Czechoslovakia, Tunisia and several Latin American countries. Greenpeace has over 4.5 million supporters, allowing it to operate in complete independence from commercial or government ties.

Greenpeace ships and inflatables are now recognised across the globe as a potent symbol of environmental protest. Greenpeace currently operates a fleet of eight ocean-going vessels and many small, fast and highly manoeuvrable inflatable dinghies — the kind used by Greenpeace to shield whales or harass large ships carrying poisonous waste across the sea. The flagship, *Rainbow Warrior*, is a sail-assisted converted deep sea trawler capable of sustaining long voyages across the world's greatest oceans.

Greenpeace is still inextricably bound up with the sea, and it is therefore highly appropriate that this book, *The Sea*, should be dedicated to the work of Greenpeace. The wealth of material within these pages is a true celebration of the wonders of the sea, and together Greenpeace and *The Sea* serve to remind everyone of the many threats facing the marine environment.

Irish rock band U2 join Greenpeace in protest at Sellafield reprocessing plant (*Greenpeace/Morgan*)

Greenpeace driftnet action in the North Pacific (*Greenpeace/Dorreboom*)

MV Greenpeace in Canada

As whale blood sluices from Japanese whaling factory ship, Greenpeace protests at the slaughter (*Greenpeace/Culley*)

The Sea: A CELEBRATION

Shell
ANDREA TANA

Underwater life
GRAHAME BAKER

Dolphin in Dingle
Hearing tales about a friendly wild
dolphin in Dingle on the south west
coast of Ireland I travelled down. The first
sight of this graceful, elegant ambassador
of the sea up close had a lasting
impression. Since that time I have spent
all my holidays, weekends and snatched
days off floating in an inflatable in the
middle of the bay waiting and have often
been granted a visit from a dolphin. Even
the times between visits have not been
unfulfilling as I have grown to love the
sea for itself, not an empty prairie but a
shimmering, chameleon wilderness
hidden beneath a lapping canopy
SEAN MANNION

Painting taken from The Sand Horse
(Anderson Press)
MICHAEL FOREMAN

The Sea

Feckless, faceless, fathomless sea,
Turbulent temptress torturing me.
Treacherous, tedious, testing, tyrannical,
savage, salacious, seductive, satanical,
lifegiving limitless link
Land to land, love to love, light to light —
Shall I ever cease to think —
Sea ceaselessly in sound and sight —
of sea's proud, paradoxical perversity?
Anarchic, aggressive, afflicting adversity,
Dispensing delight, dreams, delusions and danger,
Murderous, mystical, musical mood-mirror,
Hopeful, hateful home to me,
cringing, cunning, cleansing sea.

DR JOHN deCOURCY IRELAND

15

Beach; Gorton, Isle of Coll, Argyll
DENNIS DAVIS

Fred Harper's thirty-five foot Warrior III
Sickle Moon in the Firth of Clyde off the
Cowall shore near Innellan
JOHN CLEARE

Clamp the Mighty Limpet

This poem to be read in a warlike voice!

I am Clamp the mighty limpet, I am solid, I am stuck,
I am welded to the rockface with my superhuman suck,
I live along the waterline and in the dreary caves,
I am Clamp the mighty limpet, I am Ruler of the Waves.

What care I for the shingle, for the dragging of the tide,
With my unrelenting sucker and my granite underside,
There's only one reward for those who come to prise at me:
To watch their fingernails as they go floating out to sea.

Don't upset me, I'm a limpet, though it's plankton I devour,
Be very, very careful — I can move an inch an hour!
Don't you poke or prod me for I warn you, if you do,
Just stand still for a week and I will come and stick on YOU!

PAM AYRES

Rock pool, Welcombe, north Devon
ANDREW LAWSON

Under the Storm (watercolour)
P. J. LYNCH

21

Left *Flaming Dusk*
Shot from a diving vessel, this tranquil
but fiery scene makes the North Sea
appear almost tame
MICHAEL SIMMONS

*Sunset over 'Dead Man', Blasket Island,
Dingle, County Kerry, Eire*
MIKE HARDING

The Sea

The sea is not our environment. Nevertheless, the destructive potential of the human race is such that we are now having a disastrous impact on even this very much larger element. The world – the land world on which we live – has faced tyranny and genocide, plague, eruption, drought and deluge, and has survived. Even great wars have not destroyed it. But now, for the first time in the existence of *homo sapiens*, it is having to cope with what one might loosely call the *Lemming Factor*.

The world's population is now growing at the terrifying rate of 97 million per year – something that has never happened before – 184 humans are being born every minute. They all have to find food somewhere. Though not an element in which he can naturally survive, man has always turned to the sea in moments of desperation, either to carry him to some hopefully green and fertile land beyond the curved rim of the horizon, or for the sustenance of a piscine harvest.

Our interest in, and involvement with, the sea has grown considerably in the years since World War II. Our attitude to it has also changed. Until the middle of the last century, right back to the days of the Golden Fleece, and beyond, the sea was a hard, dangerous, demanding life. More and more mankind came to rely on it for the transport of goods. Navies were built to protect the trade, and great battles were fought, cannon mouth to cannon mouth.

But with the advent of steam everything changed. The world became smaller. Pelagic fleets hunted whales and seals to near-extinction, trawlers dredged the seabed, scoring out the breeding grounds. Coal gave way to oil, and with the oil came pollution on an ever-increasing scale. The rape of Neptune's dominion took on an alarming aspect – even the humble herring was in danger of going the way of the more visible seals and whales. The *Torrey Canyon*, the *Amoco Cadiz*, the *Exxon Valdez* show the damage a single tanker load of oil can do.

Among those who really care for our environment, and are not just paying lip-service to a fashionable cause, there remains a schismatic problem still to be resolved: how much of global damage is caused by man and how much by the all-powerful forces of Nature?

Thanks to scientific work mainly carried out in the Antarctic, we now know about the holes in the ozone layer. The disastrous effect of forest destruction is painfully obvious. Global warming, caused by our extravagant use of fossil fuels, appears to be raising the level of the oceans; the thickness of sea ice in the polar regions is being constantly monitored, and it is diminishing. Yet one cataclysmic eruption can alter the track of giant atmospheric storm masses. All one can say is – WATCH IT. Sea and sky, together with the bedrock below us, is what governs our future on Planet Earth. There is a natural balance. If we are too greedy, we will tip that balance, and then . . .?

HAMMOND INNES

Tynemouth

DENNIS GILBERT

Watercolour

Our road: a winding flint-blue creek.
Ploughed fields a stiff, flashing sea.
The clouds are dun-and-purple mud,
Creeks and pulks awash with sky.

KEVIN CROSSLEY-HOLLAND

Watercolour
ROBIN BELL-CORFIELD

The House on the Rock

'Therefore everyone who hears these words of mine and puts them into practice is like a wise man who built his house on the rock. The rain came down, the streams rose, and the winds blew and beat against that house; yet it did not fall, because it had its foundation on the rock. But everyone who hears these words of mine and does not put them into practice is like a foolish man who built his house on sand. The rain came down, the streams rose, and the winds blew and beat against that house, and it fell with a great crash.'

MATTHEW CH.7.V.24—27

The House on the Rock
RODNEY MATTHEWS

Emperor penguin and Weddell seal series in
watercolour and gouache
HELEN COWCHER

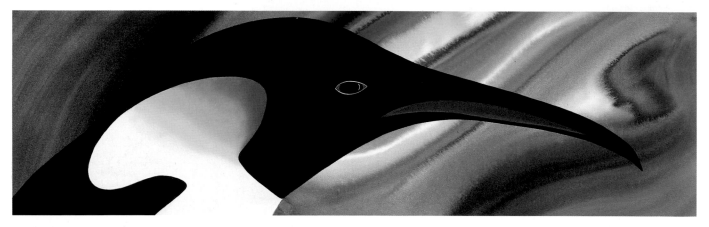

30

Turning the Tide in Cardiff

The power of the sea is awesome – but is it as powerful as a government-funded Urban Development Corporation? King Canute only tried to hold back the tide, and he knew he couldn't win. In Cardiff, there are dangerous men determined to stop the tide completely.

For a century or more, Cardiff was the coal capital of the world. The black gold of the Welsh valleys was traded there, and shipped away to fuel the furnaces of industry. Generations of dockers and sailors had their lives ruled by the rhythmic rise and fall of the tides. Now, after fifty years of sad neglect, the coal quays have collapsed, the River Taff and the River Ely have at last run clear of coal dust, and small sailing boats are moored where the iron-clad freighters used to be. All that remains of the port's proud past is a few majestic buildings, still lined with the spoils of an empire – and the tide, rising and falling, twice a day, every day without fail.

When the sunset and low water coincide, the view across Cardiff Bay is breathtakingly beautiful: 600 shining acres of mud, criss-crossed by trickling creeks, with here and there the silhouette of huge timbers that once supported waggons, cranes, and mountains of coal.

Sadly, such beauty is lost on the rat-race wheeler-dealers charged with the task of restoring Cardiff's economic wealth. They have in mind, a slick, designer image for the city: an image better served, it seems, by a static lake than a tidal estuary filled with 'ugly mud'. They deal in expensively packaged sterility – an anywhere landscape of bijou litter bins and dockland memorabilia, where quayside bistro tables offer Mediter-ranean views of blue skies and wind-surfers, and the tide is always high. £200 million of public money will buy them a barrage – a concrete dam to seal the mouth of Cardiff Bay, cut off the city from the sea, and replace the rise and fall of tides with 600 acres of still water.

Even the powerful Corporation will have difficulty suffocating nature. Cardiff's tidal estuary is alive with wading birds. Tens of thousands overwinter there, and when the dunlin and the redshank, and the dozen other species, leave each spring to fly as far afield as Greenland, or Siberia, hundreds of shelduck stay behind, to carry on the endless job of cleaning up the mud. Cardiff's rivers are still polluted. A steady flow of sewage, laced with grime, flows down into the bay. The resulting soup feeds millions of micro-organisms in the mud, and they in turn, provide the food for fish, and all those precious birds. The wealth of wildlife here is so extremely rich, that Cardiff's tidal estuary is scheduled as a Site of Special Scientific Interest and listed as a world class wetland.

If Cardiff Bay is dammed, then it is damned – the estuary's natural clean-up system will be killed, but the pollution will keep flowing. As it accumulates in the new, prestigious lake, Cardiff will be treated to a stinking soup of algal slime, topped off with clouds of midges and mosquitoes. The threat to public health will wipe out all thoughts of wind-surfing, cut off the flow of inward investment, drive out the businesses, and leave the citizens of Cardiff worse off than before.

Gazing out over the glittering mud of Cardiff Bay, and gasping at the formation fly-past of thousands of

Inspired by the wonders of the sea, a collection of ceramics
KATE MALONE

wild birds, it's hard to believe that a government and its henchmen can be so short-sighted. Here is a unique place: a capital city with world class wildlife at its heart, kept healthy by the power of nature, and costing next to nothing to conserve.

The current plans project this as a city of get-rich-quick Philistines. Surely the time has come to market development in harmony with nature; to sell Cardiff as a city of conscientious sensitivity. The planning power and the public money must be taken out of the hands of brutalisers. If the tide can turn in Cardiff and keep on turning, day in and day out, then the strength of the sea will have taught us a lesson that might just save the Earth.

CHRIS BAINES

33

The Sea-goddess

My cabinets are oyster-shells,
In which I keep my orient pearls;
To open them I use the tide,
As keys to locks, which opens wide
The oyster shells, then out I take
Those orient pearls and crowns do make;
And modest coral I do wear,
Which blushes when it touches air.
On silver waves I sit and sing,
And then the fish lie listening:
Then sitting on a rocky stone
I comb my hair with fishes' bone;
Then whilst Apollo with his beams
Doth dry my hair from watery streams.
His light doth glaze the water's face,
Make the large sea my looking-glass:
So when I swim on waters high,
I see myself as I glide by:
But when the sun begins to burn,
I back into my waters turn,
And dive unto the bottom low:
Then on my head the waters flow
In curlèd waves and circles round,
And thus with waters am I crowned.

1668

Shells Collected on a Beach in Western Australia
CHRISTINE HART-DAVIES

Pack Ice: RRS John Biscoe *makes heavy weather through the pack ice west of Adelaide Island, Antarctic peninsula*
IAN MCMORRIN

36

Iceberg
MARTHA HOLMES

Islands 4/100   Sally McLaren '90

Incubating Great Skua calling from nest
The skua is often a forgotten victim of
overfishing as it steals food and chicks
from other seabirds such as the terns.

The skua is a highly aggressive bird,
well known for attacks on anything or
anybody approaching the nest. For me,
this is just a small symbolic example of
nature fighting back
MARK MATTOCK

Arctic terns feeding chicks
MARK MATTOCK

Seawords

Sea green curtain
tumbling kelp
raised beach
protects the watcher

Rotting holdfasts
spice the air
transluscent
stones glisten

Rafts of seabirds
scatter in the wake
of the day
sheerwater

Sea sanctuary
washes the mind
inner peace
immaculate concept

Smooth as soap
we slide
body pressed
the cloud hides the moon

Rhum silence
static heron
reflections
seal the day

Oystercatchers
wave dipping
late sun
awash with joy

Crow black
weathered hull
Buckie voices
Float on the swell

Gannet splashes
on a steel sea
canisp stac polly
reflect the summer sun

Narrow sea window
boat colours
slide past
beetles in the copper sun

ROBERT CALLENDER

Seaweed — sea thong
LAURIE CAMPBELL

Compass jellyfish, inshore, Lundy Island, Bristol Channel
BOB GIBBONS

More Seals, More Fish

Seals eat fish, the popular wisdom goes, so to have more fish one should work toward having fewer seals. It seems so clear and simple and logical. The only problem with the theory is that it's wrong, so wrong, in fact, that the opposite is true.

Most Western nations with a significant commercial fishing industry have policies that involve managing, regulating, harvesting, taking, cropping, or culling seals, all of these terms being euphemisms for the bald act of killing. Some, like Great Britain, under the curiously-entitled Conservation of Seals Act 1970, permit an annual kill of 2,000 Atlantic Harbour seal pups, a figure that for all practical purposes is all the baby harbour seals on England's coasts. It takes some time, but killing all the young is an infallible formula for extinction. Combined with the outbreak of phocine distemper virus which has devastated seventy-five per cent or more of the eastern Atlantic Harbour seal population along the coasts of the British Isles, Denmark, West Germany and Holland, the Conservation of Seals Act may 'conserve' eastern Atlantic harbour seals right out of existence in Great Britain.

Some countries, like Canada, are more covert. Having ended the baby harp seal hunt with great fanfare and publicity, the Department of Fisheries and Oceans has for years quietly dispatched its wildlife biologists to study and research the diets of Harp seals and Grey seals to determine whether they are eating lobsters or commercial fish species. There are only a couple of flaws in this scenario. Neither Harp seals nor Grey seals eat during the breeding and moulting seasons, the only times they are on the ice. Instead they fast, living off accumulated body fat. The rest of the year they live at sea, and so little is known of these species, no one knows exactly where they go, which makes it difficult to hunt them down and shoot them when they are feeding.

No scientific study has ever reported Grey seals nor Harp seals eating lobster even during the nine to ten months of the year that they do feed. But since seals have refused to cooperate with the government by keeping food diaries, the only way to find out exactly what they eat is to do what wildlife biologists call 'stomach studies'. One shoots the seal and slits open its belly to examine and identify the contents. Unfortunately, the only time the seals are accessible is when they are on the ice pupping, during which time they fast so there's nothing in their stomachs to prove anything one way or the other. The scientists keep coming up, quite literally, empty. Since killing baby seals is internationally frowned upon, and pups' tummies are full of nothing but mother's milk, it is necessary to kill adult seals. Of course, shooting a mother seal kills not only her, but her baby, which starves to death, a sort of 'two-for-the-price-of-one' deal. Many of the seals shot are only injured; many more sink before they can be recovered, which means that still more adult seals must be shot to obtain a sufficient sample. In fact, government research suggests that only thirteen per cent of the seals killed or wounded are recovered. The official position, in a statement from the Department of Fisheries and Oceans, is this: 'Seals inhibit the maximization of fisheries growth potential, adversely affecting rational harvesting of these natural resources and maximization of a healthy economy. Such negative-flow factors must be dealt with by scientifically validated management programmes such as the one we are engaged in'. Under the guise of fisheries research, Canadian taxpayers are funding a seal hunt that most of them don't even know about.

The United States protects seals under the 1972 Marine Mammal Protection Act, but fishermen are permitted to shoot seals that tear nets or foul gear. Fishermen resent competition for fish in which they have a proprietary interest, which by a fisherman's definition is all the fish there are, so when the act is likely to go undetected by law enforcement officials, commercial fishermen shoot seals (Stroud & Roffe, 1979).

It's essentially the same story around the world, differing only in geographic location and species of seal. Yet even with all the killing of seals of the past two centuries, commercial fish stocks have dwindled to the vanishing point. Country after country has had to reduce commercial limits; country after country has had to shorten the commercial fishing season. In March, 1992, the Atlantic Salmon Federation issued a communiqué stating, 'Even with season adjustments, gear restrictions, prohibition of incidental catch, and quota introduction, the numbers of Atlantic salmon returning to the rivers of Newfoundland and Labrador are dwindling. Salmon stocks are nearing extinction in Newfoundland despite millions of dollars expended by the Department of Fisheries and Oceans . . .'.

Gill-nets, drift nets, bottom dredging, and centuries of overfishing have stripped the North Atlantic seas of everything but remnant fish populations. These are the same waters that 300 years ago inspired the English fishing captain, John Mason, to write, 'Cods are so thick by the shore that we hardly have been able to row a boat through them'. In 1630, Nicholas Denys described the cod in the Gulf of St Lawrence: 'Scarcely a harbour [exists] where there are not several fishing vessels taking every day 15,000 to 30,000 fish . . . this fish constitutes a kind of inexhaustible manna'. Of Riviere au Saulmon in Cape Breton, he recorded: 'I made a cast of the seine net at its entrance where it took so great a quantity of Salmon that ten men could not haul it to land and . . . had it not broken, the Salmon would have carried it off. We had a boat full of them, the smallest three feet long . . .'

Today the Canadian government is quietly buying back commercial salmon fishing licenses in Newfoundland and Labrador, in the faint hope that stopping commercial fishing altogether may allow the fish to rebuild a sustainable population. The salmon are nearly gone. The herring are nearly gone. The cod are nearly gone.

In February, 1992, The Canadian government reduced commercial cod quotas by thirty-five per cent in Canada's once-teeming North Atlantic waters — and simultaneously proposed re-introducing the Harp seal hunt and developing new seal products, including seal meat for human consumption. Fisheries Minister John Crosbie acknowledged that the predator-prey relationship between Harp seals and cod is 'not fully understood', and stated that the government will undertake a major research project to study the stomach content of seals to determine what species of fish they are eating.

Saddest of all, the evidence is that seals actually increase the numbers of fish. Many species of seals eat squid, lamprey eels, and other fish predators and parasites. Studies done on Steller's sea lions and Pacific Harbour seals in British Columbia found that their diet consists so little of salmon that the figure constitutes a negligible 2.5 per cent of the annual commercial salmon catch (Spalding, 1964). A study done on California sea lions at the mouth of the Rogue River in Oregon found that 87 per cent of their diet consisted of lamprey eels which parasitise salmon (Jameson & Fisher, 1977). Even using official Canadian government figures, grey seals eat no more than 1.6 per cent of the catch of commercially fished species; the vast majority of their diet is of fish of no commercial value. Where the Northern elephant seals pup and breed at Año Nuevo Island off the coast of Northern California, the sport fishing boats find superior fishing. In *The Natural History of Año Nuevo*, leading Northern elephant seal researcher, Dr Burney Le Boeuf of the University of California at Santa Cruz, observes that the seas are richer in algae near the seal rookery, increasing the food supply for intertidal invertebrates which are food for small fish which are food for large fish which are food for seals as well as people. By enriching the marine ecosystem and by preying on commercial fish predators and parasites, seals increase the numbers of fish substantially.

Seals mean more fish, not fewer. In *Sea of Slaughter*, Farley Mowat's book documenting the relentless commercial war against the creatures of the sea, a Canadian Department of Fisheries official is quoted: 'There's no solid proof that seals ever were a major problem. In fact, there's good evidence that, as an integral part of the marine biota, their presence is important to the successful propagation of a number of commercial fish species. Look at it this way: in the nineteenth century over twice as much cod was being landed, even with old-fashioned methods, as we can get now. And there were millions of seals out there then'. Many millions more seals then. And millions upon millions more fish.

Where wildlife populations have been protected from all hunting and killing, they have come back. The Northern elephant seal was virtually wiped out between 1818 and 1880. Protected by Mexico since 1922, and the United States since 1972, the population has grown from 125 to more than 100,000, slowly repopulating its historic range along the West Coast of North America. The same must be done with seals, whales and fish. A ten-year, internationally-observed ban on commercial fishing along the coasts of North America is the only hope that the sea and all that dwells therein can survive this century.

SARA GODWIN

Full Fathom Five
Full Fathom five thy father lies:
Of his bones are coral made;
Those are pearls that were his eyes:
nothing of him doth fade,
But doth suffer a sea – change.
Into something rich and strange.
(Shakespeare – *The Tempest*)
TONY ROBERTS

48

I saw a ship, a beautiful ship
A- sailing on the sea,
It comes from far and wide
With pretty things for thee.

TOM'S RETURN

There's fine silks to wear
Precious seeds to sow,
And caskets of jewels
All encased in gold.

There are candies so sweet
Pure spices so hot,
And China tea stored
In a wooden caddy box.

The sails are up and tied
The flag waves from the mast,
The crew shout Hooray!
As the anchor is cast.

And there, lo and behold!
Up on the deck I see,
My love who has come home
To stay and marry me.

∘ TEXT ∘ © CAROLINE ANSTEY 1992 ∘ ILLUSTRATION ∘

Sailing

I must go down to the sea again, to the lonely seas and the sky,
And all I ask is a tall ship and a star to steer her by.

JOHN MASEFIELD

The sea has always inspired people to verse and song. Now it inspires documentaries about pollution.

When you sail the seas for a living it is difficult to understand the deliberate destruction and pollution of our oceans. Everyday thousands of tons of waste is dumped into the oceans, seas and rivers and because most of us can't see it we ignore it. The people responsible for indiscriminate dumping of raw and untreated waste go on doing it. Why? Because we only complain if it affects our beaches and we can't swim from them. The problem goes so much deeper than most of us realise. Our whole food chain is in danger – we eat the fish that eat our waste products.

I have been sailing for twelve years and even in that short time have noticed the increase in pollution in the oceans and the rubbish around our shorelines. When we crossed the North Atlantic on *Maiden* we passed many floating objects such as an armchair and a fridge!

The sea took the earliest explorers to the far corners of the world. When they looked out across the ocean they saw exactly what we see. When we rounded Cape Horn on *Maiden* we saw exactly what the sailors on the first Tall Ships to round the Cape saw. The sea is as unchanging as time. A massive and complex environment that covers seventy per cent of the Earth's surface.

We cannot tame or control the sea but we could use it, carefully. The tides have the power to make electricity, wind in the sails can drive our ships and the marine life can feed us.

Our attitudes toward the sea must change completely. How will we explain to the next generation that we knew we had to do something and yet did nothing? How will they understand the ignorance and carelessness of the world's governments? The human race has achieved dizzying heights. We can send rockets into space but we cannot feed all the people. We build huge supertankers that transport our oil around the world but we still cannot deal effectively with oil spillage. Instead we all rely on small groups of dedicated but underfunded conservation organisations to campaign on our behalf. It was not the powers of the world who instigated the research into and eventual banning of whaling but the tireless efforts of Greenpeace.

Everyone can do something. The most important thing is better education for everyone on the environment and conservation. If we knew the damage that we do every day by pouring cleaning detergents down the sink maybe we would think twice – if we do not know what to do to help then we should ask. Everyone must learn that if the human race and the world in its clumsy care are to survive the sea must survive.

TRACY EDWARDS MBE

Shell
ROD HOLT

Right
The Sea Off Trevose Head
The Sea: I love its consistency, its
spontaneity, the concord between sea and
cloud; its dramatic comings and goings,
its gentle touching and falling away. It
never ceases to move me and pre-
occupies me utterly
BARBARA NEWCOMB

Left
Bosigram, west Penwith, Cornwall
Gill Cannon makes a delicate move on
'ochre slab'
JOHN CLEARE

Bridges of Ross, County Clare, Eire
JOHN FELTWELL (WILDLIFE MATTERS)

Sea chart showing the food chain (taken from Ocean World, courtesy of Mitchell Beazley)
DALE EVANS

Blue Lagoon
This panel measures 800 × 600mm.
I used hand-made mouth-blown glass
renowned for its texture, streaks and
bubbles. The border and the fish's
mouth are hand painted using glass
paint (a mix of finely levigated glass
dust, metal oxides and flux) which is
then kiln fired to fuse it with the glass
for permanence. Basically a 'cartoon'
is designed and coloured, and the lead
and glass pattern is worked out. The
glass is then cut, painted, etched or
stained and is finally leaded up and
cemented for fixing in situ
JENNIFER MILLER

Can you bear to look this whale in the eye?
This illustration was commissioned by
Penthouse magazine for an article called
'Bloody Whaling'
RALPH STEADMAN

A Conversion

Some whale supporters maintain that considerations of humanity offer sufficient reason not to kill whales. I cannot agree. No form of death is humane, and once you start to draw lines you are in terribly difficult terrain. An absolutist position — people should not kill animals — is at least consistent and defensible. But to say that we should kill fish but not whales is harder to justify. One ends up attempting to balance human need against animal suffering. Perhaps whales do have a greater capacity to suffer than, say, cattle. Perhaps people do need beef more than they need whale meat. If both statements are true then the humane argument may carry some weight, but I would not rely on it. After all, the working whaler's need for whale meat is considerably higher than anyone else's. So I do not think that the fact that killing whales may be cruel will ever stop anyone who is intent on killing whales.

There is an even more useless argument, which is simultaneously the most powerful and the most pathetic. Whales are magnificent. The largest creatures ever to inhabit the Earth, they are supremely adapted to their environment. They are beautiful in their majesty. The notion that they should die to provide lubricating oil for tanks, or margarine, or fuel for lamps, or food for dogs and cats, or hoops for corsets and crinolines, or delicacies for the palate, is repugnant. But there are so many beautiful, awesome, unique creatures that we use all the time. What is so special about whales?

This, I confess, used to be my point of view. When I first started covering the International Whaling Commission, back in 1979, I really could not see what all the fuss was about. Either whales are a bounty available for exploitation, or they are not. If it turns out that they cannot be exploited in a sustainable fashion, well, that may be bad news for the whales in the short term, but that is the way of the world. Aesthetic concerns have nothing to do with it.

Then I saw some whales in the wild.

I visited the Sea of Cortez, in Baja, California, on a whale-watching cruise, the newest way of exploiting whales. I saw Grays, Minkes, Seis, Fins and Humpbacks, not to mention vast numbers of dolphins and porpoises. At one stage our boat was surrounded by a school of about twelve Blue whales, all feeding. They were spectacular to watch, their sleek blue-grey bodies easing through the water. When a whale dived down its tail left a fluke print of still, taut water on the choppy seas, a remarkable display of strength and power.

Standing on the bridge, at one point I looked down and saw a whale's blowhole no more than four or five metres off our port bow. It breathed, with a sonorous resonating moan, and swam slowly on. I glanced back, and saw its tail fins on a level with our stern. The boat was ninety-five feet long. The whale was a few feet shorter.

Just ahead another whale crossed our path. As it did so a cloud issued behind it. Shimmering dots of red light glimmered in the sunlight, like laser beams against the deep blue of the water. The whales had been feeding on swimming crabs, known for their carotene pigments. Those pigments pass through the whale's digestive tract unchanged. Even the red shit of Blue whales is lovely.

None of this matters at all. A Blue whale may be a

spectacular sight, enough to induce an unexpected feeling of cosmic oneness in a 'hard-hearted' rationalist. But it is also 100 tonnes of meat, and just as no whaler is going to stop because it hurts the whale, no whaler is going to stop because someone else thinks his prey is wondrous.

Where does this leave us? As long as money in the bank multiplies more quickly than whales in the water there can be no hope of sustained whaling. That leaves unsustained whaling, or no whaling. Given their past history, and their current machinations, I do not think it is reasonable to expect the few remaining whalers to exercise any self-restraint. They are, I fear, likely to take the last whale they can. It may not be money alone that finally stops them. There may be greater concerns, like world standing and economic realities, but I think it would be foolish to assume that any whales will be given up while there is still a hope that they can be taken.

There is, in fact, no reason to whale. The meat forms an insignificant part of the average Japanese diet. There are substitutes available for every product of the whale. Equally, there is no reason not to whale. The protein may be unimportant, but it is favoured. The other products do have their uses. In the end, it is a question of judgement.

We have the power to take the whales, although we do not need to. We have the power to save the whales too, though we do not need to. Why not save them?

JEREMY CHERFAS

Whale Nation

From space, the planet is blue,
From space, the planet is the territory
Not of humans, but of the whale.

Blue seas cover seven-tenths of the earth's surface,
And are the domain of the largest brain ever created,
With a fifty-million-year-old smile.

Ancient, unknown mammals left the land
In search of food or sanctuary,
And walked into the water.

The arms and hands changed into water-wings;
Their tails turned into boomerang-shaped tail-flukes,
Enabling them to fly, almost weightless, through the oceans;
Their hind-legs disappeared, buried deep within their flanks.

Free from land-based pressures:
Free from droughts, earthquakes, ice-ages, volcanoes, famine,
Larger brains evolved, ten times as old as man's . . .
Other creatures, with a larger cerebral cortex,
Luxuriantly folded, intricately fissured,
Deep down, in another country,
Moving at a different tempo.

And the whale's lips formed their distant, humorous curl,
When we were clawed quadrupeds,
Insect-eating shrews,
Feverishly scrabbling at the bark of trees.

64

. . . this great and wide sea, wherein . . . there is that
Leviathan, whom Thou hast made to play therein.'

PSALM 104: 26

Whales play, in an amniotic paradise.
Their light minds shaped by buoyancy, unrestricted by gravity,
Somersaulting,
Like angels, or birds;
Like our own lives, in the womb.

Whales play
For three times as long as they spend searching for food:
Delicate, involved games,
With floating seabirds' feathers, blown high into the air,
And logs of wood
Flipped from the tops of their heads;
Carried in their teeth
For a game of tag, ranging across the entire Pacific.
Play without goals.

Naked, with skin like oiled silk,
Smooth as glass,
They move at fifty miles an hour.
Attaining faultless streamlining
By subtly changing the shape of their bodies:
Altering ridges of cartilage, and indentations of flesh
To correspond to constantly differing patterns of water;
To accommodate minute oscillations with vibrant inflexions of
muscle and skin,
So that layers of liquid glide over each other,
In an easy, laminar flow.
No drag, no turbulence.
A velvet energy.

Like Buddhists,
They are not compulsive eaters.
They can go for eight months without food;
And they do not work to eat.
They play to eat.

The Humpback catches its food by blowing bubbles.
Five-foot-wide bubbles, as large as weather-balloons:
When they burst, they make a circle of confusing mist.

The plankton: the Arctic shrimps, the krill, the sea-butterflies
Are corralled into the middle by a bewildering ring of hissing
                                        bubble bombs.

The whale then rises up
Into the centre of a round plate of brimming water,
And eats.

. . . Imagine blowing soap-bubbles,
And food drops out of the sky.

After dinner, music:
Ethereal music that carries for miles,
A siren's song,
Leading sailors to believe,
As the sounds infiltrated through the wooden hull,
That their vessels were haunted
By spirits of the deep.

HEATHCOTE WILLIAMS
Courtesy of Jonathan Cape

Left *The Stillness*
AMANDA WARD

Right *Marlin*
JANE SMITH

Original watercolour in familiar Quentin Blake style
QUENTIN BLAKE

Wooden panel, painted and carved
LINDA SMITH

69

A Brief Life by the Sea

Where I used to live they had spoiled the sea. So I moved far away, to a clean place, and I am happy here. Now waves are the only traffic I can hear. This is no place for television news; the ocean demands your attention, and lulls. It is the sound of the earth breathing.

My life here is dominated by the sea. Its sound, its smell, the shock of its chill at dawn, and the soothe of its caress on itchy afternoon skin. To walk along the slick wet flats at low tide, and be startled from contemplation by two dolphins. Laughing torpedoes surfing crystal waves. Perfect flashing steel bodies aimed along the break, racing for the thrill of speed, then knifing out the back as the peak collapses into the shore.

I live in a wooden house behind a dune, perched on the rim of the Pacific. Tiny beaches of glinting sandgrains accumulate around the doormat, and between the slate tiles on the floor of the shower. Sensation of being part of the beach.

Subtly shifting dunes dust my life with reminders; reminders that the very ground on which I walk is fluid, temporary. My house is built on sand, sand that is the property of the dunes, which rise and fall at the whim of the winds. And beyond... The Ocean. She can change from mirror calm to cyclonic fury; she builds beaches, eats bays. I am sitting on the Earth's lip, brushed by her breath.

The lady from the developers came yesterday. All smiles and a smart suit. The Resort will be built in the best interests of the community; she said. It will bring jobs, better roads. Yes there will be a small outfall, and of course, a few bins on the beach. But think of the value of your Real Estate; and she winked.

And I walked down to the water, and stood and looked out to sea. I thought of the carparks and the coke cans, and I wondered; where on Earth will I go next?

CHRIS KING

Lonely Beach
Westward Ho!, Devon
DICK JONES

Day Trip to the Whitsundays, Queensland,
Australia (oil)
CLIFFORD BAYLY RWS

Marine Life
LIANE PAYNE

'marine life'

diane Payne 1992

Left *Dolphin*
CARLTON WATTS

Low clouds, Friog Beach in May (Courtesy of
Browse & Darby, London)
DIANA ARMFIELD RA RWS

Seaing the sea

knee deep in ocean
something in the ever steady knee-cap lapping motion
of the ocean
moves me to emotion
something infinitely playful
something totally and finally benign
in the briny
make these four eyes of mine wet with weep
(as if there wasn't enough salt water already)

JOHN HEGLEY

Pastel watercolour and ink
CATHIE FELSTEAD

Poseidon
ALAN BAKER

Surf, Stanbury Mouth, north Cornwall
NEVILLE FOX-DAVIES

Dolphin collage
HAMMIE

Left   *When Puffins Play*
JOSSE DAVIS

Wave pattern
ROSS MACLENNAN

Boys Will Be Boys
Westward Ho!, Devon
DICK JONES

Pelicans Rising
CLIFFORD BAYLY RWS

Left *Waimarie — Peaceful Waters*
ANNETTE SULLIVAN

Discus Fish
Where a raised eyebrow or a tilt of the
head conveys our feelings, each fish
seemed to have shape, colour and mouth
to display their own characteristics
FARANAK

89

A Message from the Sea

We may not understand whalesong, but maybe whales can understand us. I saw something that makes me think so.

The Humpback population that migrates along Australia's east coast is recovering. In the southern winter, pregnant females and their companions head north from Antarctica to the balmy waters inside the Barrier Reef. They will not be threatened on their journey; and once in the Coral Sea, their calves can be born in safety.

As spring approaches they head south again. On their way they can sometimes be seen in the distance, from high, easterly vantage points. A sharp eye will catch their backs rising like slow grey hills from the water; and their breath blowing fine spray. They don't have much reason to come into shore.

On this occasion they did. I was on the cliffs of Cape Byron when these three came. At first they were dark patches in the distance, shifting like cloud shadows in the blue-green ocean. In less than half-an-hour they were beneath me; and by that time the cliffs were lined with people, pointing and smiling. Word travels fast.

The patch of water in which the whales can be clearly seen from the cliff tops is quite small. A couple of football pitches in a four thousand mile swim. If they kept cruising they would pass through it in a tantalising moment. But they didn't. The three of them, two adults and a calf, lingered at the foot of those cliffs for over twenty minutes.

To come close to a whale is to come close to a mystery. No statistics can prepare you for the sight of a great grey shadow rising to the surface like a blunt submarine. Adult Humpbacks are the size of buses; their pectoral fins stretch out like the wings of a small glider. It is awesome. And all the time you wonder, what are the warm thoughts behind those eyes? What are the words of the ancient songs that they sing across the shadowy depths?

On this day they stopped in clear water below a hundred or so people and rolled, one by one, their great gleaming white bellies to the surface. As they rolled slowly over, they raised their huge pectoral fins towards the sky. The fifteen-foot equivalents to the human arm, held high aloft, water streaming from them in sparkling salute. One ducked in slow motion, air rushing like wind from its lungs, and raised its tail flukes so that they spread like huge slick wings above the water. Even the little one rolled onto its back.

I can't get the image of those great long fins reaching up out of the ocean from my mind. I think they were putting on a display; I think they were waving. It might be their way of saying thank you.

CHRIS KING

Man Swimming with Whale
DANIEL LEHAN

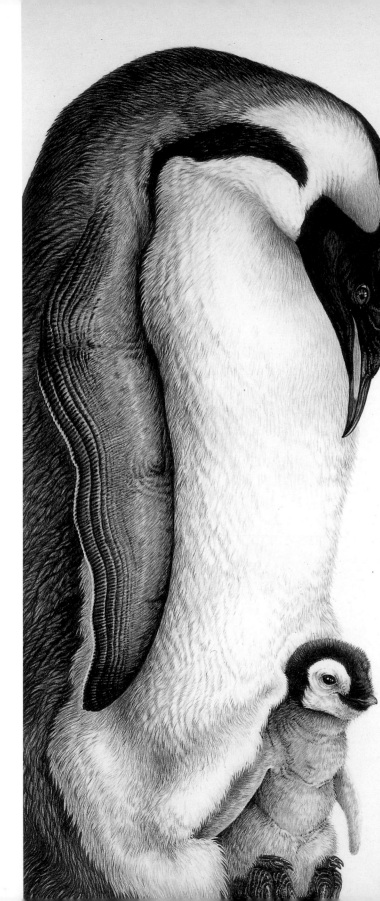

Emperor penguins
GARY HODGES

92

Polar bear in sea beginning to ice over, Cape Churchill, Canada
HEATHER ANGEL

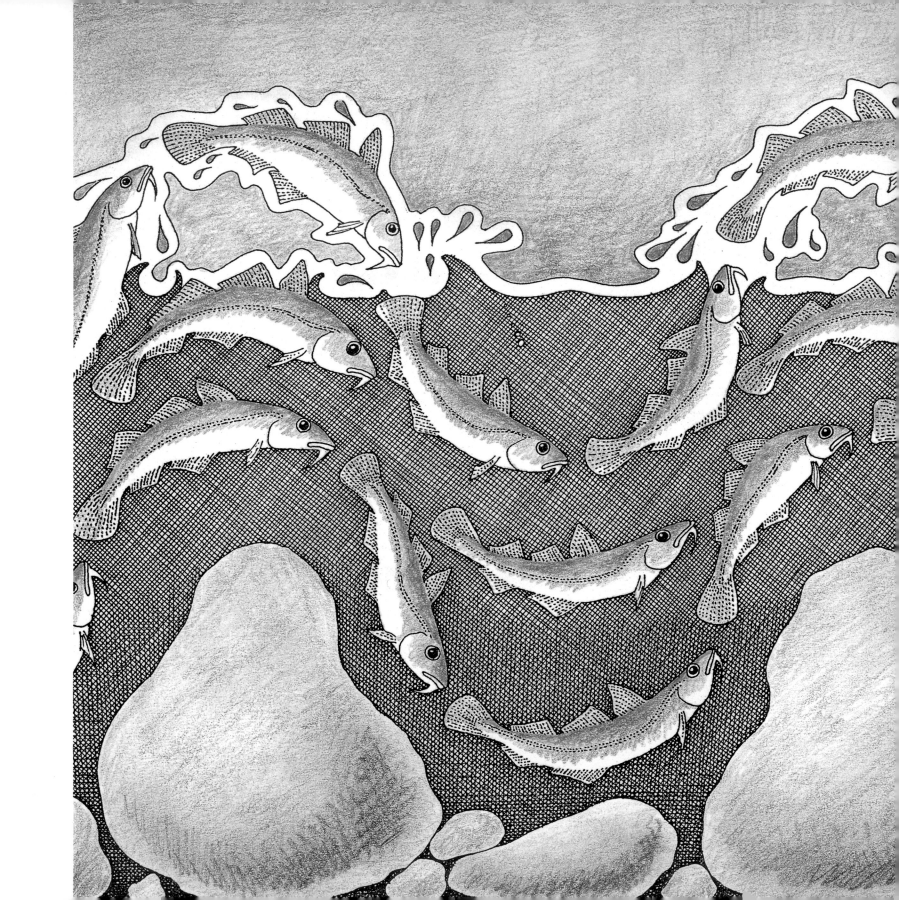

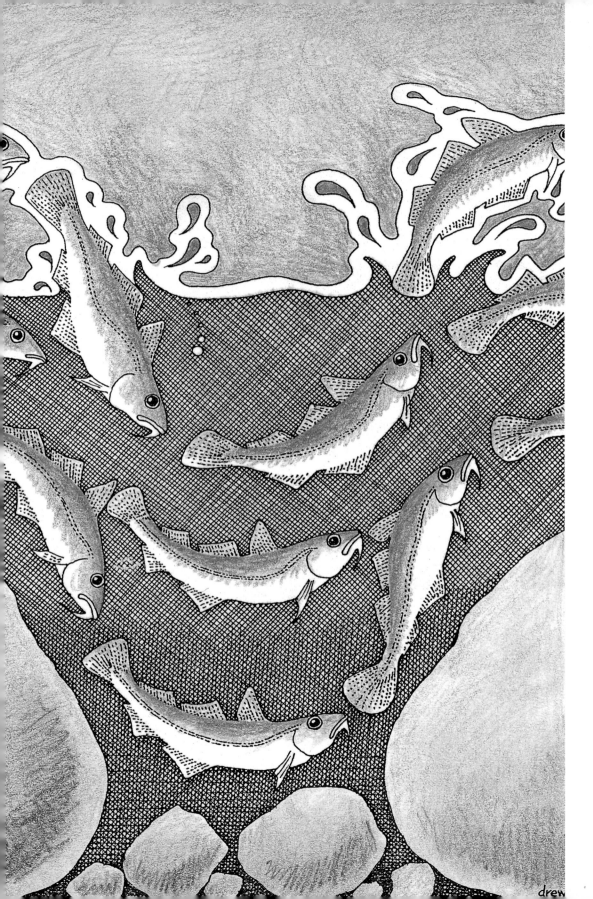

Cod Moving in a Mysterious Way
SIMON DREW

95

Sea Cow Encounter

As the boat edged its way into the umpteenth shallow channel in the mangroves, and the sun beat down on the back of my neck, I began to console myself that I had at least seen a manatee. The fact that it was more a glimpse of a torpedo shape in a swirl of mud than a face to face encounter was beside the point. Three hours of cruising the small mangrove island off the coast of Belize in search of the 'shy and elusive' creature has yielded one hazy glimpse and plenty of shredded eel grass on which these cows of the sea graze.

But then the boatman headed back out to sea and in a shallow area of water, no more than a couple of metres deep, we heard the unmistakable gasping breath of a manatee. It swam at a leisurely pace a few metres away gently wafting its rounded tail up and down. Every few minutes it would rise up to breathe with only the tip of its elongated snout breaking the water.

It seemed remarkably unfazed by our presence so I decided to take a closer look. Slipping into the warm water I pulled on my snorkel and mask and dived. A few strokes brought me alongside the manatee and we swam along together till I had to return to the surface to breathe. I spent ten minutes swimming alongside or behind the animal trying to mimic its graceful undulating progress. The high point for me was when I felt I had become an honorary manatee as we rose slowly in synchrony to breathe at the surface. My aquatic friend did not share my view and when it glimpsed me out of water took off in alarm. Perhaps like the sea cows, we are uglier exposed to the harsh light of day than the softer dappled tones of the marine world. As I pulled myself elated, back into the boat, I recognised the brown material floating everywhere that I'd been swimming through. Yes, manatees are truly the cows of the sea.

MILES BARTON

Sea Cow
MILES BARTON

Giants Causeway, County Antrim, Northern Ireland
PAUL WAKEFIELD

The Northern Coast

The fields of home for me as a child were the dairy pastures of an Irish farm. A river of salmon and trout ran to the north and my window looked north over the whiskey distillery of Bushmills to the stepped headlands of the Giant's Causeway and beyond to the grey Atlantic. On still September evenings the river mist filled the vale above the church and carried the tumble of water from where a mill race used to turn a wheel. The village was called Bushmill before its second mill was built. In the old tongue the rivers name meant 'the stream of the bursting torrents'. On its banks dwelt the poet Amergin, favourite of the high kings of Ireland, who sang of heroes and listened to the salmon.

These small things I learned as a child.

On sharp winter nights I had my father's work tending cattle in must-sweet byres. Barley straw for bedding. (Some of the neighbours grew barley for the distillery. Some, more mindful of mortal skin, thought it wasn't right.) Outside, the cold constellations astride the vast sky held me in thrall.

One winter a neighbour's tractor wheel split the capstone of a buried cist. A grave untended for 3,000 years opened to the sky. My grandfather led me to where rings of old trees hid neglected dolmens twenty times as old as the trees.

At school they taught us victors' names and dates, the profits of empires in tonnes of bananas, and the dry balancing of mathematical equations empty on either side. A mile down the road from the classroom, the seamen's cottages lined the shore. They were strangers who talked with foreign-sounding words like 'glashen' and 'gurnet'. Farmers eat salt fish no more than fishermen gather potatoes. Two miles from the sea, I never learned to swim, but I could stand for hours in the dark theatre of sea cliffs watching the grey swell breathing under a heavy moon.

I asked my teacher why the sea was blue. She told me it reflected the sky. I asked her why the sky was blue. I think I first left my home and my fields to find out why the sky was blue.

In all our lives we grow to recognise ourselves more certainly year by year. We learn what simple things give us pleasure and how their absence leads to illness, pain or anger. Our forefathers, neighbour by neighbour, also knew these simple things, the essentials of contentment, knew them through necessity for without them they quite literally could not live. They understood their seasons, they understood their soils, their crops, and they understood that their lives were inseparably connected with them. Their own daily lives were made their songs, and their dances weaved through harvest sheaves where young-blood feuds and romances were encompassed within a village hall. Their first ancestors marked the spoor of deer they hunted and knew the woodland glades where elderberry, blackberry and hazelnuts grew, and measured the days until each returned in their different seasons. In the memories of our own families often our lives have been lived in different fields again where the soil has been hidden by concrete and we have measured our time and sold it by the hours of a factory clock.

Now, from my window, on the steady land the plough returns each time to the headrig and turns. Shallow scratches approved by their straightness each harvest erased with cutting bars and threshers with the sweet smell of tea in the tin can. Bleak runnels in cold

November rain seep to sheughs that swell and flood the river meadows. The people of this place, we dip our mills in the river of life and grind from the stone what we can. Running up the headland the blast from the dangerous sea holds me braced above the cliff whilst below the edge of the vast ocean plunders the basalt rock. Between the black cliffs and the white cliffs, the glorious, plunging waves drown the wails of Cuchulainn over his slain son, dead by his own red hand; drown the saintly prayers of Patrick on high Dunsevericks rock; drown the splintering of the Armada treasure on the black dykes of Port na Spaniagh; drown the shrieks from grand Dunluce as the banqueting hall slides below the air; drown the cries from Casements soul, still lost in Murlough Bay; drown the rantings and ravings and the bullet cracks and all giants and the little men are tangled, thrashed upon the shore. And as I count toward the seventh wave the quiet deep salmon move home across the vast Atlantic toward the mouth of the River Bush and, amongst the fields we know, four white swans alight on the water meadow and we wait for them to sing.

DAVID LYONS

Wreck of the Eliza Johanna
DAVID LYONS

Sea Lions
CHARLOTTE LYON

St Katherine Dock was opened on 25 October 1828, the first ship to enter was the Elizabeth, the subject of a painting by William John Huggins (1781–1845). With its historic atmosphere and interesting vessels it is still inspirational to artists of today
TERENCE STOREY

Left *Fisherman, Eastern Point Lighthouse,*
Maine, USA
DENNIS DAVIS

Venus rising in Pisces
Ecologically the two fish can be seen to
symbolise balance (yin/yan), with Venus
as the pleasure principle derived from
achieving such equilibrium
SHAWN RICE

Rock pools
MICHELLE ROSS

From Jack Scout

We look out there over the lip
of the earth and see
only the beginning
of the sea's uplifted gift —
the alchemical drama
screened on our skin of sky.

Down here the sea's gone
out, cleansing the gut
of our gastric earth —
the infections of cities,
the urine of factories,
the additives of agriculture.

Down here the sea's gone,
leaving these alimentary
canals to shelduck and curlew
feeding under the living
wind-patterns of water,
the slow patterns of sand.

Out there the sea's coming
back as a long cascade
of white light washing in between
the nuclear ulcer of Heysham
Power Station and the gallstone
of Vickers at Barrow from which

one day submarine explosions will rupture the sky.

TERRY GIFFORD

From Jack Scout
JULIAN COOPER

III

Walrus beach off the Siberian coast in the Arctic
COLIN MONTEATH

The Legend of Skye
KAREN HIRST

Journals from a sea sanctuary (Ink charcoal
photograph)
ELIZABETH OGILVIE

In the wake of the poisoned wind
DERMOT SEYMOUR

Dead Water

IAN MILLER

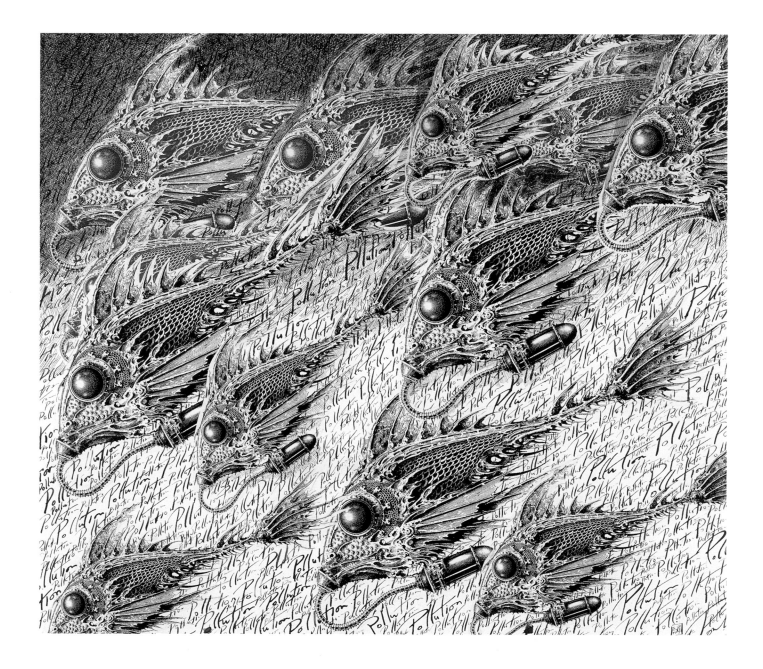

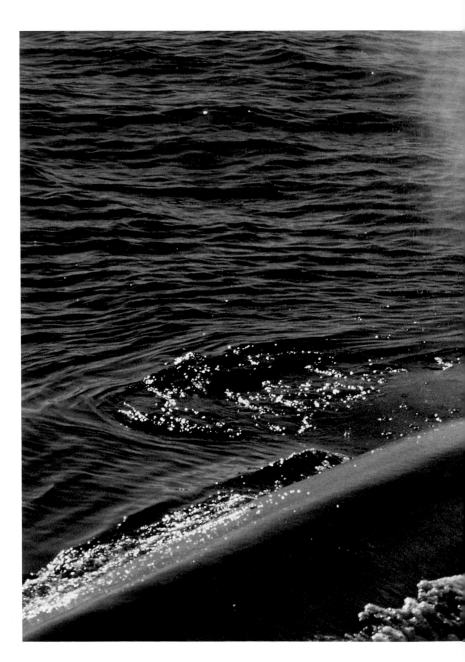

Blue whale showing blow hole, Sea of Cortez,
Baja, California
HEATHER ANGEL

Who cares?

We all know that wildlife usually comes a distant second
to commercial interests and politics. But, sometimes, it
even gets lost in the rush to deal with other environmental issues. After all, the extinction of a few animals or
plants can seem almost irrelevant compared to major
problems like global warming or the destruction of the
ozone layer.

If those creatures live underwater, in the depths of
some unexplored sea, their survival can seem even less
signficiant. We lull ourselves into a false sense of security
by believing that, somehow, the sun will still rise in the
morning – even if we stand by and watch one species
after another becoming extinct. Nature, we think, will
cope with the damage and cover up our mistakes. So we
continue to overfish, to throw toxic wastes into the sea
and to hunt whales and seals until they disappear.

But the fact that we have 'got away with it' so far
should not make us complacent. Nature's resilience is
remarkable – but there is a limit to how far it can be
stretched.

Most important of all, there is more to conservation
than just the struggle for survival. It is about caring. And
there is no better reason for protecting Giant Clams,
Mediterranean Monk Seals, Blue Whales or any other
species than the fact that the world would be a poorer,
darker, lonelier place without them.

MARK CARWARDINE

Adelie Penguins, Hope Bay, where the Antarctic Sea meets land
PAUL MORRISON

121

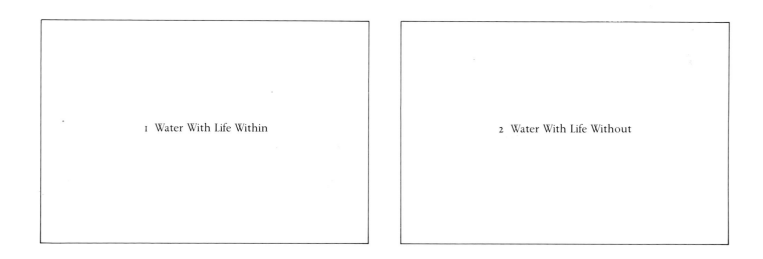

1 Water With Life Within   2 Water With Life Without

Ballyferriter Bay Sunset, Dingle Peninsula, County Kerry, Eire
EDMUND NAGELE

The Contributors

NORMAN ACKROYD is an award winning landscape artist whose work is widely collected and exhibited.

CARRY AKROYD is a screenprinter, illustrator and painter. She exhibits regularly. Her work is landscape-based and she works in very small editions.

HEATHER ANGEL is one of Britain's top natural history photographers. She runs her own photographic agency, Biofotos, from her home in Sussex, England.

CAROLINE ANSTEY is a freelance illustrator. Her work is used in many areas, her most successful being children's book publishing.

DIANA M. ARMFIELD ARA, RWS, NEAC is a well known painter in oils, pastels and watercolour. She exhibits regularly and has painted in the kitchen garden of HRH Prince of Wales.

PAM AYRES is a humorous poet and TV personality.

Professor CHRIS BAINES is a horticulturist, landscape architect, writer, broadcaster and environmental advisor. He is an active campaigner for wildlife in towns and a prize-winning author.

ALAN BAKER is a freelance illustrator. He writes and illustrates his own children's books and teaches at Brighton Art College, England.

GRAHAME BAKER graduated from the Berkshire College of Art and Design in 1984. He is a freelance illustrator working mainly for design groups and is currently working on his first children's book due to be published in spring 1994.

MILES BARTON is a writer and broadcaster who works for the BBC Natural History Unit in Bristol.

CLIFFORD BAYLY RWS is a respected artist whose work has been exhibited widely. His work has been published in many areas and features the landscapes and seascapes of places he has visited.

ROBIN BELL-CORFIELD is an artist and illustrator. He has published a number of books and exhibited widely and is currently commissioned by the National Trust.

QUENTIN BLAKE is an award-winning illustrator of children's books, including books by the late Roald Dahl.

PETE BOWMAN is an established illustrator/designer and author of a number of successful children's books.

ROBERT CALLENDER is an artist whose inspiration is the sea. He uses objects found while 'beachcombing' as the basis of his work. He has exhibited widely and his work is to be found in a large number of collections.

LAURIE CAMPBELL is a natural history photographer and author, specialising in Scottish wildlife and landscapes.

MARK CARWARDINE is a zoologist, writer and photographer. He is the author of many wildlife and conservation books, has worked for several international organisations and contributes to TV and radio programmes.

JEREMY CHERFAS is a biologist and journalist with a long standing interest in conservation and sustainable living. He wrote *The Hunting of the Whale* (Penguin) after a decade of covering the worldwide conflict between conservationists and whalers.

JOHN CLEARE is a photographer who specialises in worldwide mountain/landscape photography. He runs his own agency – Mountain Photography – which features his own pictures and that of selected photographers.

JULIAN COOPER is the third generation of a family of Lake District watercolour artists. He studied at Lancaster Art College and Goldsmith's College. He lives and works in the Lake District.

HELEN COWCHER is a painter, illustrator and author. The natural world inspires her work in which she combines a sense of poetic drama with factual accuracy. She has published a number of picture books and exhibits regularly to raise funds for environmental groups.

KEVIN CROSSLEY-HOLLAND is a professor of English, a poet, writer, broadcaster, teacher and interpreter of the northern world. He has a deep interest in myth, legend and folk tales.

DENNIS DAVIS is a freelance photographer/writer specialising in agricultural and architectural subjects. His work has been widely published.

JOSSE DAVIS is a ceramicist and artist. He has his own studio at his home and when he is not working he photographs his first love – nature.

JOHN deCOURCY IRELAND has had an affinity with the sea since he walked out of school to join a cargo ship. Since that time he has devoted his life to maritime concerns in his native Ireland. He has published a number of books and has been awarded decorations for his services to a number of marine and maritime institutions.

SIMON DREW is a freelance artist and designer whose distinctive work is sold through a number of outlets including his own gallery. His work appears on cards, prints, porcelain, earthenware and stoneware.

TRACY EDWARDS MBE is a writer and sailor who was the captain of the all-female crew of *Maiden* in the Whitbread round the world race.

FARANÁK was born in Iran and came to England to study graphic design and illustration. Since graduating she has spent several years experimenting with different techniques.

CATHIE FELSTEAD studied graphic design and illustration and now works as an illustrator in publishing, advertising, set design and editorial. She has worked for a number of clients and Lynx the anti-fur group.

DR JOHN FELTWELL FRES, FLS, C BIOL, MI BIOL, DIP AFE, is a conservationist, ecologist, author and broadcaster. He runs the Wildlife Matters photographic agency from his home in Sussex.

MICHAEL FOREMAN is one of Britain's best known children's book illustrators. With many books and exhibitions to his credit he continues to produce his colourful and distinctive illustrations.

NEVILLE FOX-DAVIES trained as a graphic designer and worked in magazine and book publishing. He was an Art Director for highly-illustrated non fiction books for over twenty years before retiring in 1990. His use of the camera evolved from an interest in image making.

SARAH FOX-DAVIES is an illustrator, who studied graphic design and illustration at Hornsey School of Art, England.

BOB GIBBONS is a photographer who runs his own photo library, Natural Image, which stocks a wide range of pictures covering the natural world.

TERRY GIFFORD is a poet and lecturer at Breton Hall College. Has *The Stone Spiral* (1987) and *Outcrops* (1991) available from Littlewood/ Arc.

DENNIS GILBERT is a freelance photographer whose work covers a variety of areas, including architecture, buildings and landscape.

SARA GODWIN MA is a prize-winning, internationally published author who writes frequently on ecology and natural history. She travels the world researching her many books, magazine articles and television scripts. She lives in California.

BRIAN GRIFFIN is a photographer of wide repute who runs his own 'Produktion' company working in a variety of media including photography and video.

HAMMIE has designed for Greenpeace for over five years and uses recycled materials for much of her artwork.

MIKE HARDING is a singer, composer, comedian, traveller and photographer. He has made many TV appearances and travelled far with his own brand of entertainment.

JOHN HARRIS is a freelance illustrator. He considers his work to be imaginative landscapes, from mainstream to science fiction and fantasy. He was the first British artist commissioned by NASA.

CHRISTINE HART-DAVIES RMS FSBA HSF is a botanical artist, illustrator and miniature painter working wherever possible from life. A committed conservationist, she sees her work as celebrating and encouraging the protection of nature.

DAVID HATFIELD trained at St Martins School of Art, London, England, and went on to become a freelance commercial photographer. His work has been exhibited widely.

JOHN HEGLEY is a widely published poet who has appeared on TV.

JOHN HESELTINE is a freelance photographer. He runs his own picture library specialising in landscape, travel and food from around the world.

KAREN HIRST studied fine art and printmaking, and exhibits her work regularly through galleries and exhibitions. As well as printmaking she is currently involved in painting and drawing and more recently glass etching.

GARY HODGES SWLA works exclusively in pencil, drawing wildlife. His work has been used in limited editions, calendars, cards and exhibitions for many conservation organisations. In 1992 he produced the first ever national ITV telethon print.

MARTHA HOLMES is a writer and broadcaster who has co-hosted the highly praised BBC programme (and book) *Sea Trek*. She has travelled much for her work with the BBC Natural History Unit and has many photographs of her experiences.

ROD HOLT is an artist who was born in Saltburn-by-the-Sea, England. He studied fine art at Winchester at Sheffield School of Art.

HAMMOND INNES is an internationally renowned, bestselling author.

DICK JONES is a civil servant and a member of the Royal Photographic Society. His work has been exhibited widely.

CHRIS KING is a zoologist and writer. He has travelled widely and worked on a number of wildlife and conservation projects.

JO LAMB studied textiles and painting at Camberwell School of Arts and Crafts, England. Her paper mosaics, graphics and paintings have been used by many conservation and environmental groups.

ANDREW LAWSON trained as a painter, but makes his living from photographing gardens and plants, amongst many other things. He lives in Oxfordshire.

DANIEL LEHAN studied at the Winchester School of Art, England. He is a children's book author and illustrator and designer of T-shirts, cards and ceramics. He is also a children's workshop leader.

P. J. LYNCH is a successful illustrator whose pictures have graced many products including children's books.

CHARLOTTE LYON exhibited at the Portal Gallery, London, before moving to France for eight years. During the summer of 1991 she had a very successful one-woman show featuring images of groups of wild animals.

DAVID LYONS is an award-winning photographer whose work has been featured in numerous publications. He lives in Cumbria, England, where he runs his business Event Horizons.

SALLY McLAREN is a freelance artist, who trained at the Ruskin School of Art, England, and won a French Government Scholarship. She has taught etching, had a number of solo exhibitions and exhibited all over the world.

IAN McMORRIN is a freelance photographer whose work encompasses many natural subjects. His photographs are available through Mountain Photography.

ROSS MACLENNAN spent a number of years travelling the world taking photographs. He now runs the Employee Involvement Consultancy for Royal Mail.

KATE MALONE is an artist whose ceramics and pots are inspired by the wonders of the sea.

SEAN MANNION is a journalist with the Irish Press Newspaper in Dublin. He spends much of his spare time floating on an inflatable in the middle of Dingle Bay waiting for the sight of a dolphin.

RODNEY MATTHEWS is a respected 'fantasy' artist whose work has been featured in books, on record covers and calendars.

MARK MATTOCK is a wildlife photographer and Design Director of *Arena* magazine.

IAN & JENNIFER MILLER are the driving force behind the Miller Partnership. Artists both, they work in a variety of fields including illustration (Ian) and stained glass (Jennifer). Their work is featured in a number of publications.

COLIN MONTEATH is a freelance photographer whose work is available through Mountain Photography.

PAUL MORRISON is a wildlife photographer, author and lecturer. He runs his own natural history photo library, Natural Selection.

EDMUND NAGELE is a Fellow of the Royal Photographic Society. He runs his own photographic agency, Communications in Photography.

BARBARA NEWCOMB was born in the USA and lives in London, England. After many exhibitions on both sides of the Atlantic she has perfected the monoprint technique.

ELIZABETH OGILVIE is an artist who draws inspiration for much of her work from the sea. Her work has been exhibited widely and is featured in many collections.

LIANE PAYNE studied fine art and printmaking and now works in a variety of media. She has run her own fashion design company, and now works as an artists' agent.

LINDA PITKIN started diving in 1979 and took up underwater photography a year later. She is much travelled in the pursuit of diving and photography. Her work has been published in numerous books and magazines and she has won many awards in national and international events.

SHAWN RICE is an illustrator whose work has appeared in many areas, including children's books. She comes from Jamaica and is currently living in London.

TONY ROBERTS is a freelance illustrator working for publishing, advertising and film. Originally trained in fine art, he is now spending more time on his painting.

MICHELLE ROSS SBA is an illustrator specialising in detailed watercolours from her North York Moors studio, England.

DERMOT SEYMOUR is an artist who lives in the west of Ireland. He has exhibited throughout Ireland, USA, Canada, Finland, Belgium and Britain.

MICHAEL SIMMONS is an Australian manned-submersible pilot. His photographs display many unique ocean environments, both under and above water.

JANE SMITH is a freelance illustrator who exhibits regularly. Her techniques include linocut, collage, mixed media and watercolour.

LINDA SMITH is a freelance illustrator of books and magazines, and for advertising.

JEREMY STAFFORD-DEITSCH has a degree in philosophy from the University of London, England, where he also studied zoology. He has published two books on marine natural history subjects and is working on a third. He is interested in wildlife photography, marine conservation and natural history in general.

RALPH STEADMAN is a distinguished cartoonist and illustrator, who has won many awards for his work which has been published and exhibited widely.

TERENCE STOREY is a marine, landscape and industrial artist working in oils and watercolour. His work has been exhibited widely and features in a number of permanent collections.

ANNETTE SULLIVAN is a New Zealand designer who has designed merchandise for a number of organisations. She has her own range of hand-painted environmental T-shirts.

ANDREA TANA is an artist who works in a variety of media. Her design work includes ceramics, prints, fabrics and interiors.

CLARE WAKE began painting seriously at the age of six. She later studied painting and her work has been exhibited widely. In addition to her painting she decorates houses, illustrates books, teaches, makes painted furniture and plays the violin.

PAUL WAKEFIELD has been a photographer for over eighteen years – working commercially through design groups and advertising agencies. He has had four books of landscape photography published.

AMANDA WARD is a painter and illustrator. Her work is used on book covers, advertising and design, and she works regularly for *Cosmopolitan* magazine. She exhibits regularly in the Royal Academy summer exhibitions.

CARLTON WATTS is an artist and Christian living in Wales. He runs a successful T-shirt company, featuring his own and other artists' designs.

HEATHCOTE WILLIAMS is the bestselling author of a number of epic poems that evoke his own views on world conservation issues.

PETER WOOD is a Communications Manager for Royal Mail who spends his spare time painting, taking pictures and compiling books.

INDEX